1973
/Nineteen Seventy Three

David Simpson & Richard Callaghan

MYYear

MYWORLD
PUBLISHING

Designed by **courage**

ISBN: 978 1 901888 70 6

First Published 2013
Published in Great Britain by:
My World
Chase House
Rainton Bridge Business Park
Tyne and Wear
DH4 5RA
Tel: 0191 3055165
www.myworld.co.uk

My World is an imprint of Business Education Publishers Ltd.

British Cataloguing-in-Publications Data.

A catalogue record for this book is available from the British Library

Printed in Great Britain by Martins the Printers Ltd.

1973
/Nineteen Seventy Three

COMMON MARKET

On **January 1, 1973,** Britain became part of the EEC, the European Economic Community, popularly known as the Common Market, along with Denmark and Ireland. They joined the original six members: France, Belgium, Luxembourg, Italy, West Germany and the Netherlands, which had all been members since the EEC was formed in 1957.

Britain's attempts to join the EEC in 1963 and 1967 had been denied largely due to the resistance of the French President Charles De Gaulle, but this time they were successful. Some Britons were suspicious of the move, but Prime Minister Edward Heath was delighted and would go on to consider it the greatest achievement of his career.

First of The Summer Wine

The BBC TV series *Last of the Summer Wine* made its debut on **January 4, 1973,** with a pilot episode called, 'Of Funerals and Fish'.

The idea came from BBC Head of Comedy Duncan Wood who employed writer Roy Clarke to the task.

The plot centres on the antics of three elderly unmarried men in the last summer of their lives, though the original working title of the comedy was, 'The Library Mob'.

The original cast featured Bill Owen as Compo, Peter Sallis as Norman Clegg and Michael Bates as Cyril Blamire.

Last of the Summer Wine proved popular with BBC audiences and ran for an astonishing 31 series with the last episode broadcast on August 29, 2010.

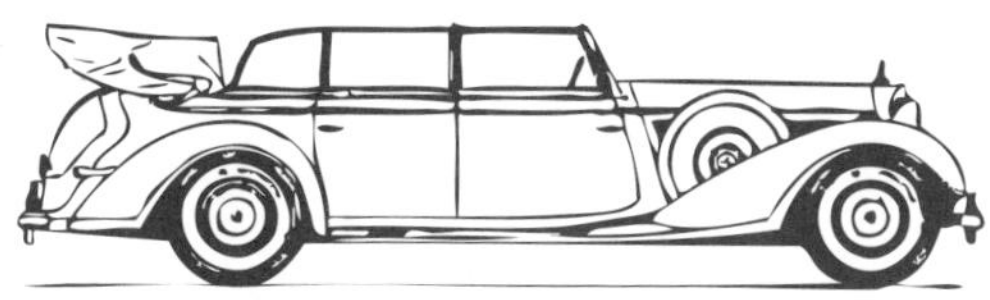

'Hitler Car' Breaks Record At Auction

A luxury vintage Mercedes 770 Cabriolet that was allegedly the parade car belonging to Adolf Hitler, was sold at auction in Arizona for $153,000 on **January 6, 1973**. At the time this was the most money ever paid for a car at auction.

The car had belonged to the Marshal of Finland, Gustav Mannerheim. The belief that it had previously been Hitler's parade car, most likely came about from a 1951 movie about Rommel that featured the car serving this role.

The car was purchased by American businessman Earl Clark for the Dutch Wonderland theme park in Pennyslvannia.

 Cuauhtemoc Blanco /
17 January 1973 / Mexican football player

Crispian Mills /
18 January 1973 / English musician, lead singer of Kula Shaker

Oscar De La Hoya /
4 February 1973 / American boxer

Kate Thornton /
7 February 1973 / British television presenter

Claude Makelele /
18 February 1973 / French international footballer

Peter Andre /
27 February 1973 / Australian singer and television personality

Jack Davenport /
1 March 1973 / English actor

Edgar Davids /
13 March 1973 / Dutch international footballer

Marc Overmars /
29 March 1973 / Dutch international footballer

Kris Marshall /
1 April 1973 / English actor

Jamie Bamber /
3 April 1973 / English actor

David Blaine /
4 April 1973 / American magician and illusionist

On **January 11, 1973,** The Open University awarded its first ever degrees.

The University, which had been established in 1969 and admitted its first students in 1971, was an attempt by the government to increase opportunities for people who previously didn't have access to university education.

Out of the 1,000 people who took the final exams, 867 of them successfully passed, and gained their degrees.

Since its foundation, The Open University has become the biggest university in Britain, with more than 40,000 students studying from home.

ROE V WADE?

On **January 22, 1973,** the US Supreme court made a historic ruling when it decided that the government had no right to prohibit abortion. By a vote of 7 to 2 it was decided that abortion was a private matter of personal choice as determined in the fourteenth amendment of the US Constitution.

The ruling was the result of the landmark ROE V WADE case in Texas, involving plaintiff Norma McCorvey (under the pseudonym Jane Roe) and Henry Wade, the Dallas County District Attorney.

An animated TV series featuring the furry, litter-tidying residents of London's Wimbledon Common, *The Wombles* was first broadcast on **February 5, 1973**. The first series, based on children's book characters created by Elizabeth Beresford in 1968, was narrated by Bernard Cribbins and consisted of 30 episodes. The last episode of the series was broadcast on July 6, 1973.

A second series of 30 episodes, again featuring Cribbins' vocal talents followed in 1975. Tomsk, Orinoco, Wellington, Bungo, Uncle Bulgaria and Madame Cholet became household names on British television.

Little Jimmy Osmond	/ Long Haired Lover from Liverpool / 19 December 1972
The Sweet	/ Blockbuster / 23 January 1973
Slade	/ Cum on Feel the Noize / 27 February 1973
Donny Osmond	/ Twelfth of Never / 27 March 1973
Gilbert O'Sullivan	/ Get Down / 3 April 1973
Dawn	/ Tie a Yellow Ribbon Round the Ole Oak Tree / 17 April 1973
Wizzard	/ See My Baby Jive / 15 May 1973
Suzi Quatro	/ Can the Can / 12 June 1973
10CC	/ Rubber Bullets / 27 June 1973

Several major strikes hit Britain during 1973.

On **February 7,** a one day general strike hit Ulster in protest over the internment of two Protestants accused of murdering a Catholic. The whole province was brought to a standstill. Public transport ceased, shops closed and all major industries including power supplies stopped operating.

Industrial disputes concerning pay hit the British mainland in mid-February when the gas workers went on strike. By the end of the month rail workers and civil servants were striking.

On May 1 the TUC called a one day strike in which 1.6 million people took part.

On November 13, power station workers and coal miners went on strike, with an overtime ban reducing coal supplies to power stations by 40%.

THE SIEGE OF WOUNDED KNEE

On **February 27, 1973**, the town of Wounded Knee, South Dakota was occupied by 200 members of the American Indian Movement (AIM). They took over the town in protest after their failed attempt to impeach tribal President Richard Wilson. Their protests were also about more general issues, including, the negative treatment of Native Americans by the US government and demands that the US should reopen negotiations with the Indian nations. The siege which resulted lasted until May 5, finally ending in a ceasefire, with many of the AIM's grievances remaining unresolved.

It was the eighth album released by British rock band Pink Floyd, but for many **The Dark Side of the Moon** was the most memorable.

Recording took place at Abbey Road Studios in London and was completed in January 1973 ready for release on March 1. It only stayed at number one in the US charts for a week, but it stayed in the charts until 1988 for a staggering 741 weeks. That's longer than any other album in history.

Selling over 50 million copies worldwide, in the UK it was the sixth best-selling album of all time with more than 3.9 million sales earning it a 9 x Platinum certification even though it never peaked higher than number 2 in the album charts. In France it was the fifth biggest selling album ever with 2.5 million sales, and it has the distinction of being New Zealand's most successful album ever.

THE NORTHERN IRELAND REFERENDUM

On **March 8, 1973**, a referendum was held in Northern Ireland which asked the people of that province if they wished to remain part of the United Kingdom or join with the Republic Ireland.

An overwhelming 98.9 % of the voters said that they wished to remain in the United Kingdom. However members of the Catholic community were requested by their political leaders to boycott the vote and the BBC estimated that less than 1% of Catholics turned out for the vote, limiting turnout to just 58.7% of voters.

In **March 1973,** archaeologists uncovered one of Britain's most remarkable Roman finds at the fort of Vindolanda near Hadrian's Wall.

At first mistaken for wooden shavings, one excavator peeled apart two thin pieces of what seemed to be unremarkable thin pieces of postcard-sized wood to reveal ink writing inside.

It was the first of the Vindolanda Tablets to be discovered and would provide a remarkable insight into communication and society in Roman Britain. More followed and by 2010, 752 of these tablets had been translated.

Dating from the first and second century AD, these tablets include an invitation to a birthday party written around 100AD which is thought to be the oldest surviving document written in Latin by a woman.

In a poll of viewers of a 2003 BBC TV documentary Our Top Ten Treasures, the Vindolanda tablets were voted the nation's favourite archaeological treasure.

The Seven Ronnies

In 1973, BBC2 aired a series of seven different comedies entitled *Seven of One*, all starring Ronnie Barker. Each was aired as a potential pilot for a new series; two eventually became established comedy series'.

As part of this series **March 25, 1973,** saw Barker star for the first time as Arkwright alongside David Jason's Granville in the pilot of *Open All Hours*, a comedy set in a grocery store.

Written by Roy Clarke, *Open All Hours* would not be broadcast until 1976. Further series would follow with the last episode of the fourth and final series broadcast on October 6, 1985.

On April 1, 1973 the pilot of *Porridge*, initially called 'Prisoner and Escort', written by Dick Clement and Ian La Frenais, starred Barker as prison inmate Norman Stanley Fletcher.

Three series of *Porridge* were made with the last episode of the final series broadcast on March 25, 1977.

The 45th
ACADEMY AWARDS

27th March, 1973 Presents ...

Best Picture
The Godfather

Best Director
Bob Fosse
Cabaret

Best Actor
Marlon Brando
The Godfather

Best Actress
Liza Minnelli
Cabaret

Best Supporting Actor
Joel Grey
Cabaret

Best Supporting Actress
Eileen Heckart
Butterflies Are Free

Red Rum

The Australian horse, Crisp, ridden by Richard Pitman had led almost all the way at the Grand National of **March 31, 1974,** and, as it safely jumped the final fence at Aintree, it led by 15 lengths.

However, in the end it was Crisp's hot pursuer the Irish born gelder Red Rum, ridden by English jockey Brian Fletcher, that finally pipped Crisp to the post by three quarters of a length, securing a record time to boot.

It was the beginning of a dream for Red Rum. He would be back the following year to win the National again before finally achieving the unthinkable third Grand National win in 1977, following two second places in '75 and '76.

As a fitting tribute, when Red Rum died on October 18, 1995 at the age of 30 he was buried alongside the finishing line at Aintree in Liverpool, where his grave can still be seen.

(+VAT)

On **April 1, 1973**, the British government played what was probably the worst April Fools' joke of all time, by introducing Value Added Tax (VAT) to Britain. Starting out at 10%, it rose to 15% in 1979, and then 17.5% in 1991. It was reduced to 15% in 2008, by then Chancellor Alastair Darling, but George Osborne increased it to 20% from January 2011.

NEW FACES

ITV's talent show *New Faces* was launched on **April 2, 1973,** and saw budding celebrities perform in front of a panel of expert judges including Mickie Most and Tony Hatch.

The series, which ran until April 1978, and was revived between 1986 and 1988, would go on to launch, or at least reinvigorate, the careers of a number of celebrities including Lenny Henry, Michael Barrymore, Joe Pasquale, Roy Walker, Victoria Wood, Roger De Courcey (with Nookie Bear), Les Dennis and Showaddywaddy.

On **April 4, 1973**, the World Trade Center opened in Lower Manhattan, New York. At the time of their construction, the Twin Towers of the World Trade Center were the tallest buildings in the world, with the North Tower being the tallest, capturing the title from the Empire State Building before losing it in 1974 to the Sears Tower in Chicago.

PICASSO IS DEAD

On **April 8, 1973**, Pablo Picasso, the man considered to be the most influential artist of the twentieth century passed away at his villa on the outskirts of Mougins in France at the age of 91.

Sculptor and painter Picasso was born in Spain on October 25, 1881. He was the co-founder, along with Georges Braque, of the avant-garde art movement known as Cubism, as well as the creator of some of the world's most famous artworks, including *Les Demoiselles d'Avignon* and *Guernica*.

Roberto Carlos /
10 April 1973 / Brazilian footballer

Adrien Brody /
14 April 1973 / American Academy Award winning actor

Sachin Tendulkar /
24 April 1973 / Indian international cricket legend

Marcus Brigstocke /
8 May 1973 / British comedian and comedy writer

Natalie Appleton /
14 May 1973 / Canadian singer, part of All Saints

Josh Homme /
17 May 1973 / American rock star and record producer

Noel Fielding /
21 May 1973 / English comedian

Dermot O'Leary /
24 May 1973 / British television presenter

Christian Vieri /
12 July 1973 / Italian international footballer

Monica Lewinsky /
23 July 1973 / American former White House intern

Kevin Phillips /
25 July 1973 / English international footballer, European golden boot
winner

Kate Beckinsale /
26 July 1973 / English actress

On **April 30, 1973,** US President Richard Nixon appeared on TV and denied any personal involvement in the bugging of the Democratic Party headquarters at the Watergate offices in Washington in 1972.

He did however accept that ultimately he must take responsibility for what had happened. It was a bad day for President Nixon who had just accepted the resignations of four of his closest aides including his Chief of Staff and the US Attorney General.

In his broadcast Nixon spoke of his determination to be open and expose the truth about the Watergate matter and declared:

" There will be no whitewash at the White House. "

THE TOMORROW PEOPLE

The children's sci-fi series *The Tomorrow People* was first broadcast by Thames Television on **April 30, 1973**. It featured a new breed of people termed, Homo Superior, who had developed special powers like psychic abilities, telepathy and teleportation.

The characters in *The Tomorrow People* worked in a secret lab in a disused London tube station where they were assisted by a biological computer by the name of **TIM**. The series ran until February 19, 1979, with a second revived series broadcast from 1992 to 1995.

One of the most ambitious TV documentary series ever produced was first broadcast by the BBC on **May 5, 1973**. The thirteen part, *The Ascent of Man*, written and presented by Jacob Bronowski, covered subjects as diverse as man's evolution, early human migration, language, mathematics, astronomy, scientific discoveries, sex and human genetics.

The series was commissioned by BBC2 Controller David Attenborough, who had also commissioned the similarly epic 13 part documentary *Civilisation*, presented by Kenneth Clark in 1969.

Bronowski was a British mathematician and biologist of Polish Jewish origin who had a great passion for the arts. He died of a heart attack in August 1974, a little over a year after the series was broadcast.

Sunderland 1
Leeds United 0

On **May 5, 1973**, Sunderland AFC made history by beating Leeds United 1-0 in the FA Cup Final, with the winning goal coming after 31 minutes and scored by Scottish midfielder Ian Porterfield. This was followed by heroics from Sunderland's goalkeeper, Jimmy Montgomery, with a double save which is widely regarded as one of the best at Wembley. Second division Sunderland were the underdogs, whilst Leeds United were the cup holders and one of the most successful teams in the country at the time. It was the first time that the FA Cup had been won by a team containing no full internationals, and the first time in the post-War era that a club outside the top division had won the trophy.

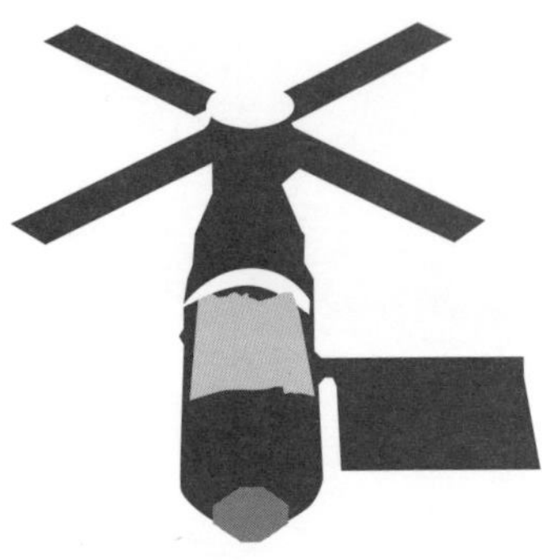

The Skylab space station was launched on **May 14, 1973,** from the Kennedy Space Centre in Florida. It was successfully sent into space by a Saturn V rocket though it did suffer some damage during the launch which threatened to cause long term damage that would make it uninhabitable.

There was no one on board when the station was fired into orbit and the first manned mission to arrive at the station on May 28 had to focus on the urgently needed repairs. Successfully fixed, the men remained in orbit for 28 days before returning to earth.

It was the first of three manned missions to the station, all of which took place in 1973. In the second mission commencing on July 28, the men stayed in orbit for 59 days and on the third commencing on November 16, the orbit lasted for 84 days.

Skylab's time in orbit came to an end in 1979 after it re-entered the earth's atmosphere and broke up, parts of the space station falling upon Western Australia.

Lambton quits!

On **May 22, 1973**, Antony Lambton, the Parliamentary Under-Secretary of State for Defence, was forced to resign after it was revealed by The News Of The World that he had been engaging in liaisons with prostitutes. Lambton resigned both his cabinet post and his parliamentary seat following the revelations, prompting a by-election, and was forced to answer numerous difficult questions about potential breaches of national security.

Virgin Records, the record label founded by Richard Branson, Simon Draper and Nik Powell, released their first record on **May 25, 1973**.

Mike Oldfield's *Tubular Bells* became a great success, and a cornerstone of the company's early growth as a record label.

Virgin Records would go on to be home to acts such as The Sex Pistols, Roy Orbison, Genesis, The Smashing Pumpkins and XTC, among many others.

"Sausages"

That's Life! hosted by Esther Rantzen was first broadcast on BBC1 on **May 26, 1973**. It focused on issues such as consumer rights and injustices, child safety and health, red tape and the service offered by various companies and organisations.

The series was not scared of mixing quite serious issues with more light-hearted and humorous features.

Presenters in 1973 included George Layton, Kieran Prendiville, Bob Wellings, Glyn Worsnip with comedic contributions from Cyril Fletcher.

Regular contributors and presenters in later years included Bill Buckley, Paul Heiney, Adrian Mills, Chris Serle, Pam Ayres, Mollie Sugden, Richard Stilgoe and Victoria Wood.

COLD WAR HOLIDAY

In June 1973, Soviet Leader Leonid Brezhnev made a rare visit by a Russian leader to the United States. Brezhnev arrived in the US on **June 16, 1973,** and stayed until June 24, holding a number of meetings with President Richard Nixon to discuss US and USSR relations.

During the stay the two men flew over the Grand Canyon where Brezhnev, a fan of Western movies, famously mimed the drawing of an imaginary gun from its holster.

On a visit to California Brezhnev met movie stars like Frank Sinatra but was particularly keen to meet Western B-movie star Chuck Connors who lifted Brezhnev off the ground in a bear hug, before presenting him with a pair of six shooters.

corruption

On **June 22, 1973**, following a long police investigation, architect and businessman John Poulson was arrested for corruption. In a case which had wide ranging repercussions, Poulson was found guilty of bribing politicians and public officials and jailed for five years, increasing to seven. He was not the only casualty, however, with high profile figures such as T. Dan Smith and George Pottinger arrested and jailed for their roles, whilst Home Secretary Reginald Maudling was forced to resign from office.

THE WORLD'S OLDEST PRESIDENT RESIGNS

The President of Ireland, Eamon De Valera resigned on **June 24, 1973**, due to old age. He was 90 years old, the oldest head of state in the world.

De Valera, born in New York to an Irish mother and father of Cuban descent, grew up in Ireland where he'd lived since the age of two.

He had taken part in the Easter Rising of 1916 and narrowly escaped execution by the British, perhaps because he could have arguably claimed to have been a US citizen.

De Valera had been president since 1959 and was re-elected in 1966 at the age of 84, making him the oldest ever elected head of state. Before his presidency De Valera had three terms in office as Irish Prime Minister between 1937 and 1959.

The British Library

Established on **July 1, 1973,** the British Library is the world's largest library in terms of the total number of objects. It holds more than 150 million items from across the world, in multiple languages, including more than 14 million books. It was originally part of the British Museum but was made a separate entity in 1973, and as a legal deposit library it contains a copy of every book published in the United Kingdom and the Republic of Ireland. More than 3 million new items are added every year, taking about 6 miles of new shelf space to house.

On **July 10, 1973,** the
Bahamas became fully
independent of Britain
but remained part of the
Commonwealth. Linden
Pindling, who had become the
country's first black premier in
1967 was the Prime Minister of
the new independent nation.
The first Governor General,
representing the Queen, was
Sir Milo Butler.

The Football League /
Won by Liverpool in Bill Shankly's penultimate year as manager, their first title in 7 years

The FA Cup /
Won by Sunderland on May 5, 1973. The Second Division team were underdogs but managed to beat the favourites Leeds United 1-0

The Epsom Derby /
Won by Morston, ridden by Edward Hide

The Grand National /
Red Rum, ridden by Brian Fletcher

Wimbledon Men's Singles Title /
Won by the Czech Jan Kodes, beating Alex Metreveli in the final

Wimbledon Ladies' Singles Title /
A victory for Billie Jean King, defeating Chris Evert

The County Championship /
Hampshire, with Surrey second

The Five Nations Championship / Now the Rugby Union Six Nations /
Finished in a five-way tie as every team won two of their games, and no further tie breaking condition was used. It was the only Five Nations Championship to end like this

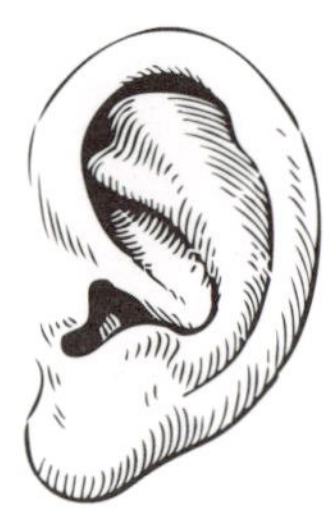

On **July 10, 1973**, John Paul Getty III, the 16 year old grandson of American oil tycoon John Paul Getty was kidnapped in Rome during the early hours. His kidnappers demanded $17 million from the Getty family.

When the ransom note arrived the demand was ignored as the young man had once joked about faking a kidnap. A second demand, delayed by an Italian postal strike, was taken more seriously but when the boy's father John Paul Getty II asked Getty senior for the money, Getty refused on the grounds that he had 14 other grandchildren and it would set a dangerous precedent.

Then, in November, the boy's ear and lock of hair were sent to a newspaper with a threat of further dismemberment unless a sum of $3.2 million was paid within 10 days.

Getty senior agreed to pay $2.2 million of the ransom (the maximum tax deductable sum) and would loan the rest to his son at 4% interest. He then managed to negotiate a deal to have his grandson released for $2.2 million.

Getty III was released in December 1973. His ear was sewn back on in 1977. He died in 2011, at the age of 54, following a long illness.

SPIDERS IN SPACE

On **July 28, 1973,** Anita and Arabella, two female Cross Spiders became the first spiders in space as they were sent into orbit on board the Skylab space station. They were sent at the request of Judy Miles of Lexington Massachusetts who as part of her student project wanted to know if spiders could spin webs in space.

The answer to Miss Miles' question was a definite 'YES', though the spiders needed a day or two to adjust to conditions. The initial attempt of Arabella, who was first to give the web-building venture a go was not too successful, but on her second attempt, the following day, she produced the first complete web in the history of space travel.

On **July 29, 1973**, Greece staged
a referendum on the abolition of
the monarchy and the creation of
a republic with a President at its
head. Since 1967 Greece had been
ruled by a military junta, initially
supported by the King, but the
King had been making overtures
to loyal members of the military
in order to organise a counter-
coup. To guarantee their position
the military junta organised a
referendum to declare a republic
and remove the King, emerging
victorious with 78.6% of the
tightly controlled vote.

THALIDOMIDE

On **July 30, 1973,** Distillers, the drug company which had marketed thalidomide in Britain, was forced to pay £20 million in damages to the children who had suffered birth defects because of the controversial drug. Pregnant women had been advised to take the drug, allegedly developed as an antidote to nerve toxins such as Sarin gas, in order to counteract the effects of morning sickness. However the drug had caused birth defects in the children, leading to a lengthy court battle with the companies responsible. In the end £6 million was paid in direct compensation to victims, with a further £14 million being put in a fund for the children's future.

Slade	/ Skweeze Me, Pleeze Me / 26 June 1973
Peters and Lee	/ Welcome Home /17 July 1973
Gary Glitter	/ I'm the Leader of the Gang (I Am) / 24 July 1973
Donny Osmond	/ Young Love / 21 August 1973
Wizzard	/ Angel Fires / 18 September 1973
The Simon Park Orchestra	/ Eye Level / 25 September 1973
David Cassidy	/ Daydream / 23 October 1973
Gary Glitter	/ I Love You Love Me Love / 13 November 1973
Slade	/ Merry Christmas Everybody / 11 December 1973

EXIT THE DRAGON

1973 saw the release of Bruce Lee's final movie, and the one for which he is probably best known, Enter the Dragon. Bruce Lee died on **July 20, 1973**, with the film being released in Hong Kong on July 26, and in America on August 19. It is a seminal martial arts movie, and was regarded as one of the key martial arts 'break out' movies. It was made for a budget of just $850,000, but grossed $25 million in the US and $90 million worldwide. The stuntmen for the movie included martial artists who would go on to great success in their own right, including Jackie Chan and Sammo Hung.

LOST FOR WORDS

Two literary giants passed away in September 1973, both of whom were inspired by the Norse sagas of ancient times.

On **September 3, 1973,** J.R.R Tolkien, author of *The Hobbit* and *The Lord of the Rings*, died in Bournemouth aged 81.

A Professor of Anglo-Saxon and English at Oxford, Tolkien was noted for his knowledge of Norse and Anglo-Saxon literature, history and mythology.

The poet, W.H. Auden, a former pupil at Oxford, once wrote to Tolkien:

I don't think that I have ever told you what an unforgettable experience it was for me as an undergraduate, hearing you recite 'Beowulf'. The voice was the voice of Gandalf.

Only weeks after Tolkien's death Auden himself passed away in Vienna on **September 29, 1973,** aged 66.

Known as, 'The Voice of the Thirties', the York-born Auden believed he was of Icelandic descent. The Norse sagas, were an important influence in his work. The lead mining landscape of Weardale in County Durham was another source of inspiration for Auden, who also lived for many years in the United States.

DNA

Gene splicing, a major breakthrough in genetic engineering, took an interesting turn in the autumn of 1973.

Biologists Herb Boyer and Stanley Cohen of the University of California took DNA from two quite different organisms - a bacteria and an African Clawed frog. They then recombined them to produce what has been described as, 'the first recombinant DNA organism'.

Births / **Vera Farmiga /**
10 August 1973 / American actress

Filippo Inzaghi /
9 August 1973 / Italian international footballer

Jay Jay Okocha /
14 August 1973 / Nigerian international footballer

Andrew Lincoln /
14 September 1973 / English actor, star of This Life,
Teachers and The Walking Dead

Ioan Gruffudd
10 October 1973 / Welsh actor

Neve Campbell
3 October 1973 / American actress

Mario Lopez
10 October 1973 / American actor and television
presenter, A.C. Slater in Saved By The Bell

Ryan Giggs
29 November 1973 / Welsh international footballer

Monica Seles
2 December 1973 / Yugoslavian born tennis player

Tara Banks
4 December 1973 / American actress, model and
television presenter

Paula Radcliffe
17 December 1973 / British long distance runner

Stephanie Meyer
24 December 1973 / American author best known for
the Twilight series

THE YOM KIPPUR WAR

1973 saw the fourth major conflict in Israeli history, as Israel and an Arab coalition led by Syria and Egypt went to war. The war, which began with a massive Arab offensive against Israel, lasted from **October 6** to October 25, and ended when, after a hugely successful counterattack, Israeli forces were just 25 miles from Damascus and 63 miles from Cairo. The Yom Kippur War greatly heightened tensions within the region and across the globe, with the Soviet Union and the United States supplying and supporting the Arab and Israeli sides respectively.

spiro to go!

In what proved to be a difficult year for the Nixon administration, the US Vice President, Spiro Agnew, resigned on **October 12, 1973,** after agreeing not to contest charges of tax evasion.

Agnew was under investigation relating to charges of evading tax and accepting and extorting bribes during his time as Governor of the State of Maryland. Agnew was fined $10,000 dollars and placed on probation. Following a plea agreement he was spared prison, but had no choice but to resign.

He was replaced as Vice President by Gerald Ford, the leader of the Republicans in the House of Representatives and the future 38th President of the United States.

On **October 16, 1973**, OPEC, the Organisation of Petroleum Exporting Countries which included Iraq, Iran and Saudi Arabia increased oil prices by 70% in protest at the United States' support for Israel in the Yom Kippur war.

From October 19, some of the OPEC nations, beginning with Libya enforced a complete embargo on oil exports to the US which was quickly extended to other nations who were considered to be supporting the US in the war.

In November, the OPEC nations announced a massive 25% cut in production, putting severe pressure on the economies of the United States and the EEC.

Britain was not subjected to the full embargo, partly due its refusal to allow US forces to use air bases in the UK and Cyprus, but the British economy still suffered from the rising oil prices.

October 19, 1973, saw the release of *Quadrophenia*, the sixth album by rock band The Who. It was The Who's second rock opera, after *Tommy* in 1969. *Quadrophenia*, set in mid-1960s London and Brighton, and discussing social, political and musical themes from a teenage perspective, was a critical and commercial success, reaching #2 in both UK and US charts. It is widely regarded as one of The Who's finest albums, and indeed regularly features on lists of the greatest records of all time.

THE DALAI LAMA IN BRITAIN

On **October 20, 1973,** Tenzin Gyatso, the fourteenth Dalai Lama, made his first visit to Britain on the last stop of his tour of Europe. During his ten day UK visit he would meet the Archbishop of Canterbury, emulating his audience with the Pope in an earlier part of the European tour.

The Dalai Lama had fled from Tibet, by then part of China, in 1959 and since that time he had lived in exile in India. He was keen to stress that his tour was not of a political nature and he refused to be drawn into discussions about Tibetan independence.

The Sydney Opera House officially opened on **October 20, 1973**. One of the most admired examples of twentieth century architecture the Opera House on Bennelong Point in Sydney Harbour is one of Australia's most iconic landmarks.

The unique design consists of several shell-like structures made of precast concrete, coated with cream coloured tiles from Sweden.

Construction of the opera house began in March 1958 to the winning design of Danish architect Jørn Utzon whose submission was one of 233 entries, in a competition launched in 1955.

Though known as an opera house, the building serves many roles; it is home to ballet, classical concerts, drama productions, lectures and meetings.

In 2003 the building was awarded the Pritzker Prize, architecture's most coveted honour.

There was one conflict which raged throughout 1973, a conflict which saw major European nations facing off against one another, a conflict which could justifiably be described as decidedly fishy!

THE SECOND COD WAR

The Cod War of 1973 saw the Icelandic coast guard cut the nets of British fishing trawlers in waters around Iceland. This had led to the dispatching by Britain of large tugboats, followed by Royal Navy warships, to protect British fishing boats from attack by Iceland.

The Second Cod War concluded on **November 8, 1973,** with an agreement which saw Britain entitled to catch 150,000 tons of fish until 1975.

At which point the Third Cod War began.

ETHERNET

November 11, 1973, saw a major leap forward in computer technology as Robert Metcalfe and David Boggs, working for Xerox at their Palo Alto Research Centre (PARC), became the first people to invent Ethernet.

Xerox was working to produce the world's first laser printer, and they wanted to be able to print documents on the printer from any computer at PARC. With this in mind, Metcalfe and Boggs developed a system to network all of the computers on the site, a system which became an industry standard and which was integral in powering the personal computer revolution.

They had met at the Munich Olympics in 1971, where he received a gold medal in an equestrian event. In March 1973, there were rumours but she denied the romance and then on May 29 their engagement was announced.

WEDDING OF THE YEAR

On **November 14,** the big event came with perhaps as many as 100 million people watching the wedding at Westminster Abbey of Princess Anne, 23, and Lieutenant Mark Phillips of the Queen's Dragoon Guards, 25.

Anne wore a Tudor style wedding dress, while her new husband wore the scarlet uniform of his regiment. Later that day the crowd cheered as the Princess and her military man kissed on the balcony of Buckingham Palace.

The marriage lasted until 1989, with the couple finally divorcing in 1992.

On **December 8, 1973**, in response to the oil crisis, the government imposed a 50 mile an hour speed limit on British roads in order to limit fuel consumption while oil supplies to Britain were restricted. The national speed limit had been 70 mph since the mid-1960s, and was kept at 50 mph until March the following year, on motorways, and until May, on other roads.

Henry Kissinger, who became US Secretary of State in September 1973 after previously serving as a National Security adviser, was awarded the Nobel Peace Prize on **December 10, 1973**.

The award was made for his efforts to secure peace in the Vietnam War. The prize was also jointly awarded to North Vietnamese politician Le Duc Tho, who refused to accept it.

Kissinger and Duc Tho were the principal negotiators at the Paris Peace Accords which concluded in January 1974 and were a major step towards bringing about peace in Vietnam.

The Prime Minister of Spain, 70 year old Admiral Luis Carrero Blanco, was assassinated on **December 20, 1973,** in a car bomb attack in Madrid. His bodyguard and driver were also killed in the attack.

The blast was so great that it threw the car over the roof of the church where Blanco had just attended mass. The bomb had been planted in a specially dug tunnel beneath the road outside the church. Blanco was a close friend and confidant of General Francisco Franco, the Spanish Caudillo.

The assassination was carried out by members of the Basque separatist group ETA.

December 25, 1973, saw the release of The Sting, a movie featuring Paul Newman and Robert Redford as confidence tricksters Henry Gondorff and Johnny Hooker, who plot to con mob leader Doyle Lonnegan (played by Robert Shaw) in an elaborate betting hoax.

Set in 1936 Chicago, the movie features ragtime music compositions by Scott Joplin which were actually composed between 1900 and 1910. The Joplin tracks were adapted by Marvin Hamlisch, with the most famous being, 'The Entertainer', which serves as the movie's theme tune.

The Sting grossed $156 million at the box office and went on to receive 10 Academy Awards in 1974, taking home the Oscar for Best Picture.

First released on **Boxing Day 1973**, The Exorcist remains a seminal horror movie, one of the most successful films of all time, and is regularly cited as one of the scariest movies ever made. The Exorcist was nominated for ten Academy Awards, and grossed over $441 million worldwide. The movie was controversial for its content, but concerns were also raised about the film makers' use of semi-subliminal images to heighten the tension, with many people expressing their disquiet over the effect that such techniques could have on audiences. The movie, however, remains a classic of the genre, and an oft-cited touchstone for horror movies.

3.937 BILLION

That's the number of people who lived in the world in 1973

If you were around in 1973 apologies if we missed you out

Just in case we did. Here's the revised figure:

3.937 billion and **one** people lived in the world in 1973